OFFICE POLITICS MANIA

Printed in Singapore
by Markono Print Media Pte Ltd.

9 8 7 6 5 4 3 2 1
10 09

Copyright @ 2010 by Corporate Turnaround Centre Pte Ltd. All rights reserved. This publication is protected by Copyright and permission should be obtained from the publisher prior to any prohibited reproduction, storage in a retrieval system, or transmission in any form or by any means, electronic, mechanical, photocopying, recording, or likewise. For information regarding permission(s), write

OFFICE POLITICS

Contents

Foreword	iii
Biography	iv
Office Politics Jokes	1
H.R. Can Help: at least we hope	6
The Art of Administering Corporate Distrust	10
Turnover Inc.	12
Survival	18
Management Can Make Madness Too	24
Golf Humor: See corporations in full	45
Office Mania – Survival is Key!	47

OFFICE POLITICS

We're All Just Doormats On The Way To Other People's Success   48

Only Geniuses Wanted For Marketing Positions   51

Rise Above The Comic Circumstances   54

A Survival Manager's To Do List   58

Playing That Ole Blame Game Again   62

Office Politics   64-92

OFFICE POLITICS

Foreword

The whole notion of 'OFFICE POLITICS,' a topic even more popular now with the pervasive powers of the worldwide web, today remains as vast in scope as the business world itself. A host of blogs, online articles and numerous forms of print media –magazines as the most obvious among the later – exist for your consumption, taking you from the deadly serious to the sublime.

This piece, on the other hand, seeks the light-hearted side of the matter, making most statements while couching them in humor. We really hope you'll sit back and savor the combination of comic strip humor, thoughtful points and poetry. Hopefully, you will relate to each scenario presented –or at least the majority of them. We hope and trust you will pass them on too. Humor is always good for the soul –not to mention there's already enough straight-laced opinion giving and exposition on the topic of office politics. People remember a good laugh, and if a poignant point comes across in the process –a nugget of truth to help you survive at work, well, isn't that a better way to remember a "point well taken?"

Please grant us your feedback. That much needs to be said in all seriousness.
So now, gather a cup of your favorite beverage, sit back and enjoy the ride. We will be "traversing the globe" to smatter humor on offices from Hong Kong to California. I hope you like the flight!

Dr. Michael Teng

OFFICE POLITICS

Biography

Dr Teng is widely recognized as a turnaround CEO in Asia by the news media. He has been interviewed on the international media on many occasions on the subject of corporate turnaround and transformation such as the Malaysian Business Radio, BFM 89-9, News Radio FM 93.8, Malaysian Business Radio, Edge Radio (USA), the Channel News Asia, the Boss Magazine, Economic Bulletin, the Today, World Executive Digest, Lianhe ZaoPao, StarBiz and the Straits Times. His online seminars are broadcasted globally by Success University, SkyquestCom etc.

Dr Mike Teng is the author of a best-selling book *"Corporate Turnaround: Nursing a sick company back to health"*, in 2002 which is also translated into the Bahasa Indonesia. His book is endorsed by management guru Professor Philip Kotler and business tycoon, Dr YY Wong. He subsequently authored more than twelve management books. His first book on office politics was entitled "What we can learn from the animals about office politics" and was translated into Mandarin as well.

OFFICE POLITICS

Dr Teng is currently the Managing Director of Corporate Turnaround Centre Pte Ltd (www.corporateturnaroundcentre.com) which provides corporate training and management advisory services. He has more than 29 years of experience in distributorship management, strategic planning and operational management responsibilities in the Asia Pacific. Of these, he held Chief Executive Officer's positions for 18 years in multi-national and publicly listed companies. He spearheaded the turnaround of several troubled companies as the CEO and also advised several boards of directors of numerous distressed companies.

Dr Teng served as the Executive Council member for fourteen years and the last four years as the President of the Marketing Institute of Singapore (2000 – 2004), the national marketing association. He was on the advisory board member to Business School, National University of Singapore and School of Business, Singapore Polytechnic as well as the Doctoral Program, University of South Australia.

Dr Teng holds a Doctor in Business Administration (DBA) from the University of South Australia, Master in Business Administration (MBA) and Bachelor in Mechanical Engineering (BEng) from the National University of Singapore. He is also a Professional Engineer (P Eng, Singapore), Chartered Engineer (C Eng, UK) and Fellow Member of several prestigious professional institutes namely, Chartered Institute of Marketing (FCIM), Chartered Management Institute (FCMI), Institute of Mechanical Engineers (FIMechE), Marketing Institute of Singapore (FMIS), Institute of Electrical Engineers (FIEE) and Senior Member of Singapore Computer Society (SMSCS). He is also a Practicing Management Consultant (PMC) certified by the Singapore government.

OFFICE POLITICS

HR Can Help: at least we hope...

Don't get frustrated, at the guy who takes the credit
Don't get frustrated, but just don't forget it,
But write it all down, sticking to fact,
Then go to HR, keep calm, and speak with tact

About all that is happening, about this show stealing person
That claims your work is his, and he's the one for promotion
Tell them about the hours, days and the weeks
You toiled, and strived for that deadline you had to keep

For otherwise, your efforts will all be in vain
And the other guy, will be praised, promoted, and that will be such a pain
So don't be disheartened, or walk away in a mood
Just document the facts, and tell HR all the groove

It may seem a strange way, to protect yourself
But it is the only way, not to be left on the shelf
The office can be a rough and tough place
It is easy to lose heart, as well as face

But keep a clear head, and things will be fine
Just write things down, constantly, all the time
Remember the other guys is as ambitious as you
And will use your hard work, and maybe his to

To make himself, heard, to get himself seen
So don't feel bad, or feel that you are mean
To make sure, that you get the credit you deserve
And to make sure those fastballs don't curve

OFFICE POLITICS

OFFICE POLITICS

OFFICE POLITICS

The Art of Administering Corporate Distrust

From real government to the corporate hallway, distrust is a given. People tell lies. And, they tell them often; more often then we could ever come to terms with. So now, because of distrust, bosses often spy on their employees. Expect more of this behavior before you anticipate less of it. That being said, there's a lot more to say...

OFFICE POLITICS

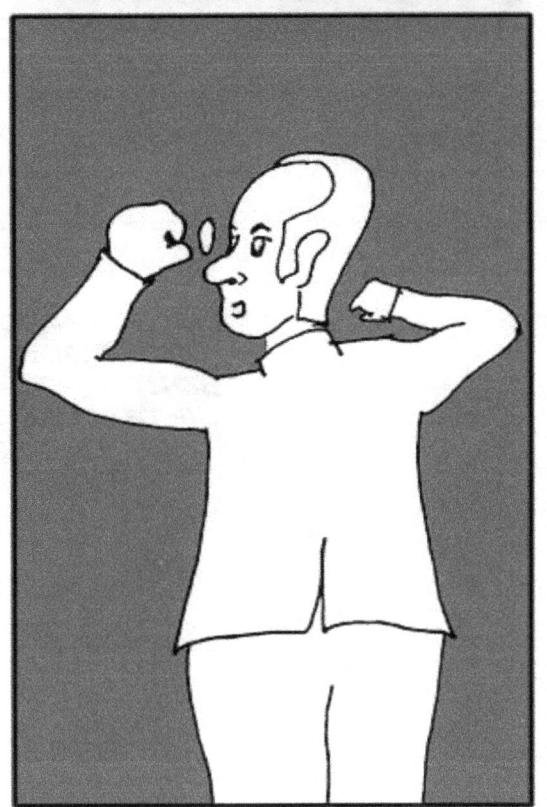

OFFICE POLITICS

"TURNOVER, INC."

> Granted, people today are not leaving their jobs as much as those days when they had more options, that is, once they decided to "move on." However, the problem now is with down-sizing, and it's a global problem. This next segment pays tribute to the person who perseveres –any way he can –to keep THAT J-O-B!

OFFICE POLITICS

Survival

The key to survive in the office environment
Is not to thrash about
with a blunt instrument
But to keep a calm head, and deal
with all things
Just remember, some will be good, or bad,
or make you sing
The world is full of different people,
but all have a goal
The world is full of different people,
with a soul
It is up to you to choose the right path
It is up to you to avoid,
being left on a raft
With books, and the guides,
the words are all around you
There are friends, there are foes,
but what's inside you
Will guide you
when things are looking a bit bleak
And with faith, and firmness,
your targets you will meet.

TOM, IF YOU'RE GOING TO CONSIDER DOING THAT, YOU MIGHT AS WELL FIND A KNIFE AND STAB HIM IN THE BACK PERSONALLY.

OFFICE POLITICS

OFFICE POLITICS

OFFICE POLITICS

Management Can Make Madness Too

Being the boss, is like walking a tight rope
Being in control, is about striking the right note
You can read all the books, read every word
On techniques, research, and the listen to all you've heard

But to make the right decision, at the crucial time
You have to throw away the books, and go with your spine
Only this way, can you make it all buzz
And get out of a hole, and get through the fuzz

If your boss is a madman, madwoman, or both
Don't get frustrated, and go for the throat
Just get to know them, and get to know their ways
As this is the best way to get on, and get a pay raise.

This may not seem true, or be the best course,
But this method is the best way, to ride the horse
Of all that happens, in a very busy company
Especially, if you're the one striving to make destiny

So don't go with the books all of the time
But listen to that voice, that speaks in your mind
As it's another a sense, like hearing or seeing
And that can help you and your company, achieve well being

Never be hasty, in judging the boss
Never be dismissive, as it will be your loss
Your pressures are different, always beware
So no charging in, tread carefully, take care.

Take the time needed, to get to know ways
Of how your boss works, as this way will pay
Learning the moods, the good, the bad,
Will only help you, feel happy and not sad.

OFFICE POLITICS

OFFICE POLITICS

OFFICE POLITICS

OFFICE POLITICS

OFFICE POLITICS

OFFICE POLITICS

OFFICE POLITICS

OFFICE POLITICS

OFFICE POLITICS

OFFICE POLITICS

OFFICE POLITICS

OFFICE POLITICS

OFFICE POLITICS

OFFICE POLITICS

OFFICE POLITICS

OFFICE POLITICS

OFFICE POLITICS

OFFICE POLITICS

OFFICE POLITICS

OFFICE POLITICS

Office mania - survival is key!

The office seems like a minefield, you have to watch every step
But there is plenty to help you, guide where you tread
The rules are a plenty, they are there to prevent
You being overlooked, or blocking that promotion event
All that matters, is your desire to achieve
All that matters, is your faith and belief
As you can face any challenge, with these qualities
With your head focused, on what everyone needs
So take heart my friend, as everything is in your hand
Your career is going, to light up the land
With every decision, every emotion you will feel
And you'll be more alive, and your soul fulfilled
So don't loose the vision or the dream
Don't loose your head, when you want to scream
The corporate world is demanding, that we all know
But you're better than mania, on your marks, get set, go.

OFFICE POLITICS

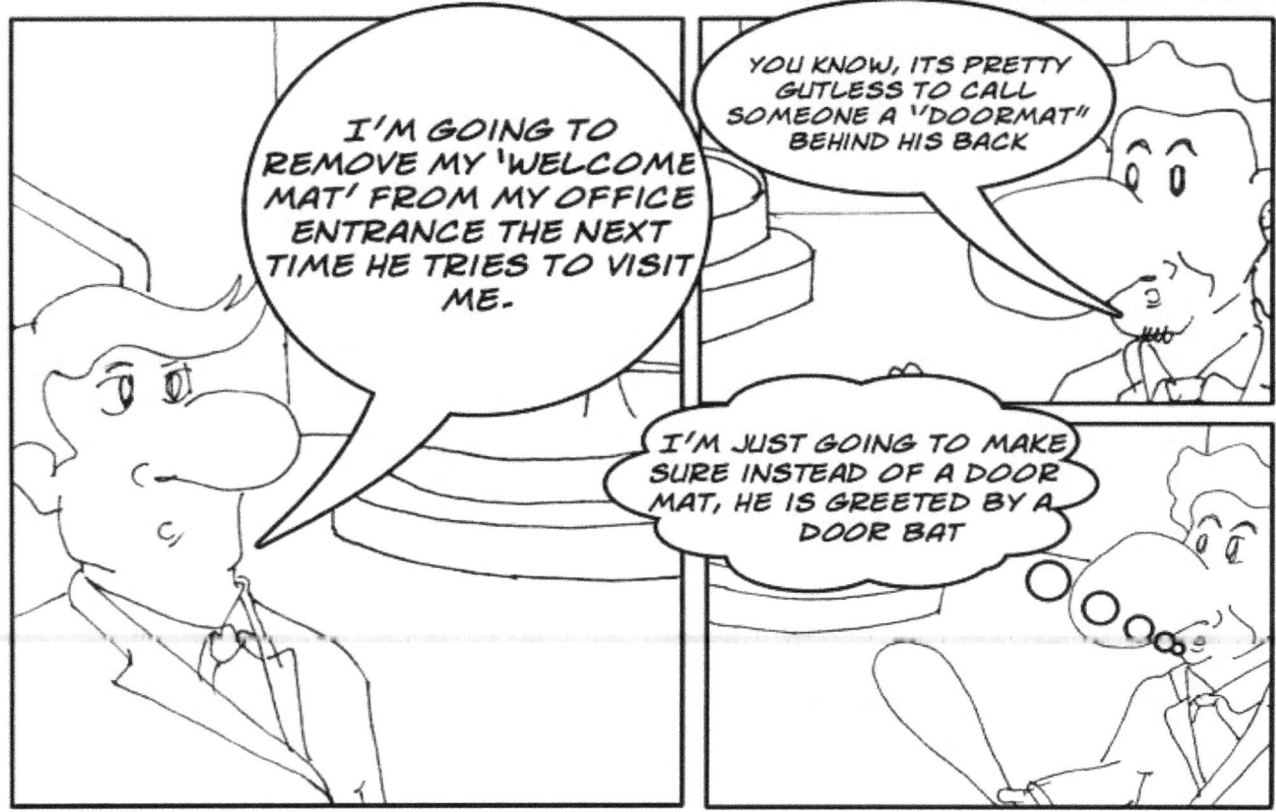

OFFICE POLITICS

"ONLY GENIUSES WANTED FOR MARKETING POSITIONS"

IF YOU HAVE NEVER INTERACTED WITH MARKETING OR INFORMATION SYSTEMS' PERSONNEL BEFORE, WELL, YOU'RE MISSING OUT ON SOMETHING. YES, YOU ARE NO DOUBT MISSING OUT ON THE CHANCE TO KEEP SEVERAL YEARS ATTACHED TO THE END OF YOUR LIFE. IN OTHER WORDS, IF YOU WORK IN EITHER OF THESE TWO AREAS YOU'RE PROBABLY ENDANGERING YOURSELF. YOU CERTAINLY WILL NEED TO COMPENSATE FOR THIS STRESS – VIA VITAMIN SUPPLEMENTS – TO PRESERVE LONGEVITY AND LIVE TO ENJOY YOUR RETIREMENT.

OFFICE POLITICS

OFFICE POLITICS

OFFICE POLITICS

OFFICE POLITICS

OFFICE POLITICS

OFFICE POLITICS

OFFICE POLITICS

"A SURVIVAL MANAGER'S TO-DO LIST"

- "Purchase surveillance cameras for office hallways"
- "Bribe other division bosses' secretary for future favors as needed"
- "Assure department members that pending job cuts won't be TOO BAD"
- "Get intern to clean and polish golf bag and clubs before big tournament next week"
- "Publish report containing wishful outcomes, for boss, instead of actual outcomes from the last disaster"
- "make sure to be on the road before 4:30 to beat rush-hour traffic going home"

OFFICE POLITICS

OFFICE POLITICS

OFFICE POLITICS

OFFICE POLITICS

OFFICE POLITICS

OFFICE POLITICS

OFFICE POLITICS

OFFICE POLITICS

OFFICE POLITICS

OFFICE POLITICS

OFFICE POLITICS

OFFICE POLITICS

OFFICE POLITICS

OFFICE POLITICS

OFFICE POLITICS

OFFICE POLITICS

OFFICE POLITICS

OFFICE POLITICS

OFFICE POLITICS

OFFICE POLITICS

OFFICE POLITICS

OFFICE POLITICS

OFFICE POLITICS

www.ingramcontent.com/pod-product-compliance
Lightning Source LLC
Chambersburg PA
CBHW060031180426
43196CB00044B/2408

A SUMMIT HISTORICAL SOCIETY PUBLICATION

DILLON, DENVER and the DAM

Sandra F. Mather, PhD.

SUMMIT
HISTORICAL
SOCIETY

Copyright © 2017- 2022 Summit Historical Society

All Rights Reserved. No portion of this book may be reproduced in any form or by any electronic or mechanical means, including information storage and retrieval systems, without permission from the publisher, except by a reviewer who may quote brief passages in a review.

Published in the United States of America by

Summit Historical Society Press
403 LaBonte Street
P.O. Box 143
Dillon, Colorado 80435

www.summithistorical.org

DILLON, DENVER and the DAM
Sandra F. Mather, PhD.
3rd edition: August 1, 2022

ISBN: 978-1-943829-45-3

Library of Congress Control Number: 2022942361

PRINTED IN THE UNITED STATES OF AMERICA

Summit Historical Society Press is an imprint of Rhyolite Press LLC
P.O. Box 60144 Colorado Springs, CO 80960

Cover Photograph: Sandra F. Mather
Book Design: Bookends Design, Boulder CO